AUSTRALIA, NEW ZEALAND AND OCEANIA
IN PICTURES

No. 2.   A Solomon Islands Canoe.

The canoe is inlaid with mother-of-pearl (refer to p. 60). The carved head on the prow is supposed to frighten away evil spirits, and to look out for reefs. Notice the large ear-ring worn by the man in front. The other man has had his hair bleached—a custom which is practised in several of the Polynesian islands, but especially in Samoa.

No. 1.   An Australian "Sundowner."

"Sundowners" are men who tramp from one sheep-run to another, doing little work for their living. They make a practice of arriving at some station at sundown, and claiming hospitality for the night. The spread of railways is helping to abolish this custom. Notice that the "sundowner" carries a blanket, and a "billy," in which to cook

Australia, New Zealand and Oceania in Pictures

BY

H. CLIVE BARNARD, M.A., B.Litt.

EXAMINER IN GEOGRAPHY TO THE COLLEGE OF PRECEPTORS AND
ASSITANT EXAMINER FOR THE LONDON UNIVERSITY MATRICULATION
AND THE NORTHERN UNIVERSITIES MATRICULATION

CONTAINING FIFTY-NINE ILLUSTRATIONS, THIRTY-TWO OF WHICH ARE
IN COLOUR, INCLUDING MAPS AND DIAGRAMS

KOOKABURRAS

(See p. 35)

PUBLISHED BY A. & C. BLACK, LIMITED,
4, 5 & 6 SOHO SQUARE, LONDON, W.1.
1923

CONTENTS.

PRINTED IN GREAT BRITAIN BY M'FARLANE & ERSKINE, EDINBURGH.

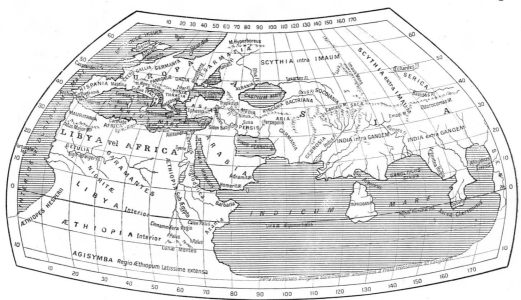

No. 3. MAP OF THE WORLD, ACCORDING TO PTOLEMY.

Ptolemy knew that the earth was a globe and that the Equator, as marked here, divided it into halves; but his map shows only those parts about which he had any information. The inscription south of the Indian Ocean means: "Unknown southern land embracing the Indian Sea from Cape Prasum to Catigara." Prasum was probably Cape Delgado, south of Zanzibar, and Catigara was a port in south-eastern Asia.

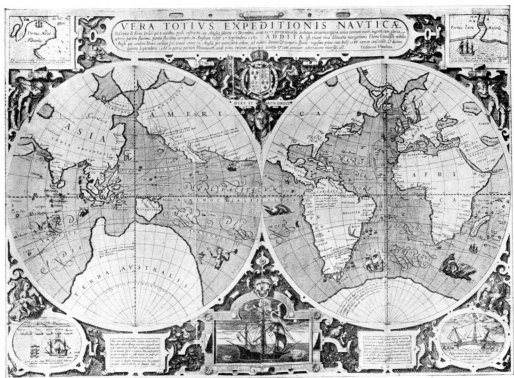

British Museum.

Artists Illustrators, Ltd.

No. 4. MAP SHOWING DRAKE'S VOYAGE OF CIRCUMNAVIGATION (1577-1580).

Refer to p. 9. Drake's route is shown by a continuous line. The dotted line indicates the course taken by Thomas Cavendish, another Englishman who sailed round the world in 1586-1588. This map, showing the results of their voyages, was published in Holland in 1595.

No. 5. ON M'KINNON'S PASS, NEW ZEALAND.

This shows a pass over the Southern Alps of New Zealand (refer to p. 50). Notice the snowfields and glaciers among the high peaks and the streams flowing down the steep rock face. The pass is named after Quinton M'Kinnon, one of the explorers of this region.

F. Wright.

No. 6. THE WAIROA GEYSER, NEW ZEALAND.

This geyser is at a place called Whakarewarewa, close to Rotorua (see p. 53). It will not spout unless it is first fed with a piece of soap; but then, as the picture shows, it throws up a jet of hot water to a great height, and continues in action for six or seven minutes.

AUSTRALASIA & OCEANIA IN PICTURES

I.—POSITION.

THE name "**Australasia**" is given to the great island-continent of Australia together with the smaller islands in its neighbourhood. They form a fifth division of the land surface of the world, distinct from Europe, Asia, Africa, and America. "Australasia" really means "Southern Asia"; and indeed we may regard it as a southern or south-eastern extension of Asia, linked on to the larger continent by the Malay Archipelago which may be compared to a broken bridge. At one time, long, long ago, the bridge was, perhaps, continuous and Australia (*i.e.* the Southern Land) was actually joined to the continent which lies to the north of it. But it is many ages ago, also, since Australia became separated from Asia, and until comparatively recent times it remained unknown and unexplored, far away in the remotest part of the world.

If you look at a globe, you will see that Australasia lies nearly opposite to Europe. If a line were drawn from London through the centre of the earth, it would come out at the surface again in the great southern ocean to the south-east of New Zealand. If two places stand exactly opposite each other on the globe, so that a line joining them would pass through the centre of the earth, each is said to be the **antipodes** of the other. If you look in your atlas you will find marked, in the ocean south-east of New Zealand, Antipodes Island. It is so called because it is very nearly the Antipodes of London.

II.—DISCOVERY AND EXPLORATION.

BECAUSE Australasia lies so far away from us on the other side of the earth, it was one of the last regions to become known to Europeans. The great civilised peoples of ancient times had never heard of it. The Phœnicians, the Greeks, and the Romans explored and colonised; but they knew as little of Australasia as they did of America. Yet some of them, who knew enough geography to realise that the earth was a globe, did guess that there might be on the south side of it another land-mass to correspond with the parts of Europe, Asia, and Africa, which they had already explored or heard about. In the second century after Christ there lived at Alexandria in Egypt a scientist named **Ptolemy**. He constructed a map of the world which was fairly accurate as regards the Mediterranean region, western Europe, and south-western Asia. Of course, it contained no hint of the existence of America; but it showed a great land-mass joining the southern part of Africa to the south-eastern side of Asia. This land, lying south of the equator, was called by Ptolemy the *Terra Incognita* or unknown country. You can see it marked in the upper map on page 5. We have discovered since that there is no such region and that the Indian Ocean is not a huge lake, as Ptolemy would have us believe. But we can see in his map one of the earliest hints that there might be a continent lying somewhere away on the other side of the world, although many centuries passed before this "Unknown Land" became known and explored.

More than a thousand years later than the time of Ptolemy, a Venetian traveller, named Marco Polo, journeyed across Asia to China, where he became an important person at the court of the emperor, Kubla Khan. When he returned to his native land he travelled by sea from China round the south coast of India and up the Persian Gulf. To do so, he sailed through the Straits of Malacca which separate the Malay Peninsula from the island of Sumatra. This region by this time had probably been explored by Arab navigators who, like Sindbad the Sailor, traded between Mesopotamia and the coasts of southern and south-eastern Asia. But practically nothing of the geography of these regions was known in Europe; and one result, therefore, of Marco Polo's homeward voyage was to show that the great southern continent, if it did exist, was at any rate not joined on to south-eastern Asia. In 1498—about two hundred years after the time of Marco Polo—a Portuguese, named Vasco da Gama, reached India by sailing round the Cape of Good Hope. The voyages of Marco Polo and of Vasco da Gama, therefore, together proved that Ptolemy had been wrong in making the Indian Ocean a lake. If there really was a *Terra Incognita* it must lie separate, somewhere amid the waters of the southern ocean.

By this time an important addition to the map of the world had been made by the discovery of America. Columbus and the Spanish and Portuguese explorers after him had been tracing the outlines of a new continent. But Ptolemy's suggestion as to the great southern land was still so strong that some people believed that it might be joined to the south of South America. Magellan, by sailing through his Strait, showed that there was at any rate a way through; and Drake soon afterwards was driven by a storm into the open ocean south of Cape Horn. This proved that here too the unknown continent, if it did exist, must be separated from the land farther south by a wide expanse of sea.

After Drake's voyage of circumnavigation, which lasted from 1577 to 1580, several maps were made to sum up all the explorations which had been made during the great age of discovery. One of them is shown in picture 4, and it is particularly interesting to us because it shows the shape and extent of the *Terra Australis* or southern continent according to the ideas of geographers at the end of the sixteenth century. You should compare it with a modern map of the world. Notice that many of the islands of the East Indies are fairly well known; Drake himself had sailed among them on his homeward voyage. New Guinea is known to be a separate island. This fact had probably been discovered by the Portuguese, for after Vasco da Gama had shown them the sea-route to India, they pushed farther east and built up a trade with the "spice islands" of the Malay Archipelago. But south of New Guinea the great southern continent begins, and it stretches without a break across the southern part of the world. It is well separated by sea from South Africa, but the strait which divides it from South America is a much narrower one. In short—as a Flemish geographer said about the time that this map was published—"The *Australis Terra* is maintained by some to be of so great an extent that if it were thoroughly explored it would be regarded as a fifth part of the world."

Many more years went by before that "thorough exploration" was carried out. The Portuguese were driven out of the East Indies by the Dutch, who captured their spice trade and have retained it down to the present day. It sometimes happened that the Dutch merchant ships, in crossing the Indian Ocean on their way to the Malay Islands, were driven southwards out of their course by storms. In this way Dutch captains, more or less by accident, traced out parts of the west coast of Australia. One of them even sailed along the south coast—the shores of the great Australian Bight, as we now call it—for a distance of nearly 1000 miles. But it was still thought that this country formed part of a huge continuous southern continent. At last, in 1642, Anthony Van Diemen, the governor of the Dutch East Indies, decided to find out, if possible, something more definite. He sent out two small ships under the command of a captain named Tasman. Follow their course on a map. They first sailed westward from Batavia in Java to the island of Mauritius, not far from Madagascar. Here they turned southwards and continued in this direction for three weeks. By this time they were well out in the great southern ocean, where strong gales blow from the west all the year round. So Tasman altered his course towards the east and ran before these winds for a whole month until at last he sighted land. It was the west coast of the island which Tasman named Van Diemen's land, but which we now call **Tasmania.** Continuing eastwards, he sighted land again and christened it Staten Land. This name had already been given by Dutch sailors to the coasts which they had sighted south of Cape Horn ; and it seems to show, therefore, that Tasman had an idea that the country which he had found was continuous with the lands which lie south of South America—*i.e.* that they were all part of the great southern continent. As a matter of fact, he had discovered the shores of **New Zealand.** He then turned northwards and finally reached Batavia after a voyage lasting some ten months.

You will notice that during the whole of this expedition Tasman had not sighted Australia once ; but he had certainly proved that much of the outline of the *Terra Australis*, as shown in picture 4, was wrong. Somewhere south of New Guinea there must be open ocean where once it had been thought that the land was continuous. Tasman made a second voyage of which we know little. He coasted along the northern and north-western shores of Australia itself—New Holland, the Dutch called it—but he did nothing to solve the problem of the extent of the great southern continent. After his time the Dutch made little attempt to explore these regions. They were hard-headed business men who did not care much for adventure, but who were anxious to make money by trade ; and from the reports which navigators brought home they gathered that the *Terra Australis* must be a barren land and quite unsuited to the growing of spices.

After the time of Tasman, therefore, few Europeans visited Australasian waters. Occasionally an English or French captain would coast along part of Australia ; but it was not until 128 years after Tasman's first voyage that any very definite additions were made to the map of this part of the world. In 1770 an Englishman named **James Cook** was sent out in command of a scientific expedition. Its object was to visit an island in the Pacific, and there to observe a transit of the planet Venus across the sun's disc. This was successfully carried out at Tahiti, and then Cook, in accordance with instructions which he had received before leaving England, set out to explore the southern Pacific. He sailed southwards from Tahiti, but discovered no land ; he therefore turned westwards and reached New Zealand. By sailing round the two main islands he proved that this land did not form part of a continent, as Tasman had supposed. Then his vessel, the " Endeavour," sailed westwards again for three weeks, until at last the east coast of **Australia** was sighted. Here Cook anchored in an inlet which was called Botany Bay, on account of the large number of different

NO. 8. AN AFFRAY WITH THE NATIVES.

The natives have seized a brand from a fire which Cook's men have lighted in order to boil some pitch, and have set fire to the dry grass, thus endangering the sailors' encampment. For more about these "blackfellows," or Australian natives, see p. 42.

NO. 7. COOK TAKING POSSESSION OF AUSTRALIA.

Cook in his own account of his voyage says: "After fixing a post firmly in the ground, I hoisted upon it the Union flag, at the same time taking formal possession of this and the surrounding country in the name and for the use of His Majesty King George III. We then drank a bottle of wine to His Majesty's health."

No. 9.   SYDNEY HARBOUR.

Refer to p. 45. Sydney itself is about seven miles from the open sea. The view is taken from the Botanical Gardens. The large house in the middle distance is the residence of the Governor-General. The street on the left leads to a ferry which connects with North Sydney—the town on the other side of the harbour.

G. W. Wilson & Co.

No. 10.   MELBOURNE.

Refer to p. 45. Melbourne, although slightly smaller than Sydney, has a population equal roughly to that of Liverpool. As can be gathered from the picture it is an up-to-date city. It is encircled by large public parks and gardens and is pleasantly situated on a cluster of small hills, so that from many points it is possible to obtain pleasant views of the city and its surroundings, plants which were found growing on its shores. "During my stay in this harbour," says Cook in his journal, "I caused the English colours to be displayed on shore every day, and the ship's name and the date of the year to be inscribed upon one of the trees near the watering place." A few miles north of Botany Bay is a splendid natural harbour round which the city of Sydney has since grown up (see page 45 and picture 9); but Cook did not explore it. All he says is that there "appeared to be good anchorage" there. From this point Cook coasted northwards for more than 2000 miles along the east coast of Australia, charting and exploring as he went. On one occasion the "Endeavour" ran on to the **Great Barrier Reef** (see picture 11), a long line of coral rocks which lie off the shore at a distance of from thirty to seventy miles from the land, and which extend from north to south for over 1000 miles. But the ship was saved and repaired, and Cook at last reached Cape York, the most northerly point of the eastern coast. There he landed, and in the name of King George the Third he solemnly took possession of the eastern side of "New Holland," giving to it the name of New South Wales (see picture 7).* "It is of larger extent," he says, "than any other country of the known world that does not bear the name of a continent; the length of coast along which we sailed, reduced to a straight line, is no less than twenty-seven degrees of latitude, amounting to near 2000 miles, so that its square surface must be much more than equal to all Europe." As a matter of fact, we have found since that the area of Australia itself is rather less than that of Europe; but it should be noticed that as a result of Cook's voyage the true extent and outline of this continent were very nearly known. The northern, western, and parts of the southern coasts had already been roughly traced out. Cook added to this a careful survey of the eastern coast, and proved that New Zealand was an island group lying apart in the southern ocean. In a second voyage, made between 1772 and 1774, he navigated this ocean as far south as possible. He proved that the open sea stretched far southwards, and that the frozen continent round the South Pole was very much smaller than had been supposed.

Cook's voyages, therefore, settled finally the questions raised by Ptolemy's suggestion of the *Terra Incognita*. This supposed great southern continent had at last been reduced to the huge island of Australia and the ice-covered region of Antarctica lying round the South Pole. Except for these land-masses the southern part of the world was now known to consist of a great ocean broken here and there by islands, of which the largest group is New Zealand.

* Notice that Cook called the whole of the eastern side of Australia by this name. It is now restricted to only that part of it which lies between latitudes 28° and 37° south. See page 45.

It now remained simply to fill in some of the details of the Australian coast-line which had been missed by Cook and previous navigators. A naval surgeon named Bass and a midshipman named Flinders set themselves to explore the south-eastern shores of Australia. They made several voyages in open boats. In 1798 they sailed through the Strait which now bears Bass's name, and so proved that Tasmania is a separate island. Afterwards Flinders explored the coasts of southern Australia. On an outward voyage from England he coasted along the great Australian Bight, examined Spencer Gulf, the Gulf of St Vincent, and Encounter Bay. He also sailed into Port Phillip, where, he says, " a settlement will doubtless be made hereafter." He was right, for near the shores of this bay now stands Melbourne, the second largest city in Australia (see picture 10). Not long afterwards Flinders made another voyage of discovery. Sailing northwards from Sydney, he followed Captain Cook's track and examined the Great Barrier Reef. Rounding Cape York, he sailed into the Gulf of Carpentaria, the coasts of which had not hitherto been explored. It had been thought that this gulf might possibly be connected with one of the inlets on the south side of Australia, and that thus the continent might be divided into two separate islands; but Flinders showed that this was not the case.

III.—THE OPENING-UP OF THE INTERIOR OF AUSTRALIA.

WHILE the coast-line of Australia was thus being traced out, other attempts were being made to explore the interior of the country. Not long after Cook's visit settlers had already begun to arrive at Botany Bay, and gradually other places along the east coast were colonised. Most of these early immigrants were criminals who had been banished or transported from this country. Prisons in England were often crowded and unhealthy, and it was thought that by sending some of the offenders to Australia not only would the prisons at home be relieved, but also the criminals themselves might gain a fresh start in the new country; so that when their term of sentence was ended, and they were free, if they wished, to return, they might be ready to lead a useful life again. Some, of course, were sentenced to perpetual banishment; but for them also it was better to spend their remaining years in colonising a new country rather than to languish in an English prison. If you look at the physical map of Australia, you will see that the eastern side of the continent is particularly suited to penal settlements of this kind. The coastal plain is in most cases very narrow, and is shut in between an open ocean on one side and a continuous range of mountains on the other. Although these mountains, for the most

NO. 11.   THE GREAT BARRIER REEF.

A visitor to the reef, describing the various types of coral, speaks of "some with finger-shaped projections, others with large branching stems, and others again exhibiting an elegant assemblage of interlacing twigs of the most delicate and exquisite workmanship. Their colours were unrivalled; vivid greens contrasting with more sober browns and yellows, mingled with rich shades of purple, from pale pink to deep blue."

NO. 12.   THE BLUE MOUNTAINS.

This is part of the Dividing Range behind Sydney (see p. 18); it shows the valley of the Grose—a thickly-wooded ravine leading up into the mountains. Notice the dense growth of eucalyptus trees and wattles (see p. 31), and the blue haze which veils the distant mountains and gives the range its name.

No. 13. WOOL BARGES ON THE MURRAY RIVER.

Refer to picture 38. The Murray is the most important river in Australia, although its volume tends to vary (see p. 21). At normal times more than 1500 miles of its course is navigable, and if suitable locks were constructed this course could be rendered navigable even in dry seasons. Even so, the mouth of the river would have to be dredged before sea-going vessels could enter it.

No. 14. A SILO, NEAR MILDURA, VICTORIA.

Silos are used by Australian farmers in order to keep green fodder fresh during years of drought or scarcity. This is done by storing it in a receptacle which is practically airtight and allowing it to ferment a little. The word *silo* really means "pit," and the vegetation to be preserved is often closely-packed and buried; but tub-shaped silos made of wood or brick or concrete are also used. Notice on the left the cutter for chopping up the fodder, and the elevator which carries it into the silo. In Britain potatoes and other root crops are often stored in silos—usually of the pit type.

part, are not very high, they are very difficult to cross—especially just behind Sydney where the earliest convict settlements were made. Many of the valleys which lead into the range end in abrupt cliffs, which can be climbed only with the greatest difficulty. Occasionally a prisoner from the coast would escape and get away into the hills. It was thought by some of these men that if they could cross the range they would reach China; which shows how little they knew about the geography of this region. Most of them died in the attempt to win freedom, and many returned, ragged and starving. But it is just possible that some did manage to find a way across the hills.

At the same time attempts were being made by ordinary explorers to discover what was on the other side of the mountains. In 1813 a party of three adventurers managed to cross the range, and reached a point from which a well-grassed and well-timbered lowland could be seen, stretching away into the mysterious distance. Other explorers made there way into this country and brought back enthusiastic reports as to its fertility and possibilities. They also found rivers running westward, and by degrees the courses of these were traced out. The **Macquarie, Lachlan, Murrumbidgee,** and **Darling** were all explored, and during the years 1829 and 1830 an officer named Sturt, who had served under Wellington in Spain, followed the Murrumbidgee down to its confluence with a " broad and noble river "—the **Murray.** He continued along the course of this stream until he reached a shallow lagoon, **Lake Alexandrina,** just before the river enters the sea. This exploration completed the main outlines of our knowlege of the river-system which drains the plains in the south-east of Australia.

The central parts of Australia still remained unvisited and unknown. It was not until 1861 that the continent was crossed for the first time from south to north. In that year an expedition, headed by an Irishman called Burke, left Melbourne. It crossed the plains drained by the **Murray-Darling** system, and at last reached Cooper's Creek—a stream which flows into a great inland lake named **Lake Eyre.** Here some of the party waited, but Burke with two companions continued their journey northwards, and after about three months of wandering they reached the Gulf of Carpentaria. On the return journey provisions gave out, and the explorers reached Cooper's Creek only to find that the rest of the party had left a few hours before. They were too weak to follow at once, and lack of food and water made it very difficult to continue their march. Burke himself died in the wilderness, and only one of his companions succeeded in making his way back to Melbourne. The journey had shown that much of the interior of Australia was desert and unpromising country.

B

In the same year—1861—a more successful expedition was made by John MacDonall Stuart who crossed from Adelaide, on the Gulf of St Vincent, to the northern coast close to where Darwin now stands.   In 1870-1872 a telegraph line was laid overland from Adelaide to Darwin, roughly along the course of Stuart's journey.   Owing to the dryness of the country traversed, camels were used to carry what was necessary.   Even with their help the task proved difficult.   Sometimes the natives interfered with the work, and had to be given electric shocks before they would leave the wires alone ; while along the northern part of the line the wooden telegraph poles were eaten by white ants, and had to be replaced by iron standards. However, the work was at last successfully completed, and there is now a proposal to build a railway along the line of the overland telegraph, so as to connect Southern Australia with the north coast.

In spite of the explorations of Burke, Stuart, and many another adventurer there are, even at the present time, large areas in the interior of Australia about which very little is known.

IV.—RELIEF AND RIVERS OF AUSTRALIA.

Our account of the exploration of Australia has shown us that the continent can be divided roughly into three main regions.

(i.) Along the **east coast** and parallel to it runs a **highland**.   It is sometimes called the **Dividing Range,** because it divides the short and rapid rivers which flow eastwards into the Pacific from the longer streams which form part of the Murray-Darling system, or drain to inland lakes, or flow into the east side of the Gulf of Carpentaria.   The Dividing Range, as the map will show, contains a number of different ridges and has different names in different places.   In the extreme south are the Grampians and the Australian Alps which, in **Mount Koskiusco,** rise to 7340 feet—the highest mountain in Australia.   This is rather more than twice the height of Snowdon, but it is not sufficiently high to reach the line above which there is snow throughout the year.   Behind Sydney are the Blue Mountains, while farther north are the Liverpool and New England Ranges.   The Dividing Range continues right into the Cape York Peninsula, and its northern part lies quite close to the shore ; farther south the mountains leave room for a small coastal plain on the east side.

(ii.) West of these highlands lies a lowland district.   Its northern part is drained into and continued by the shallow Gulf of Carpentaria.   South of this region is a water-parting, linked on to the Dividing Range, and from it several streams run southward to Lake Eyre and other inland lakes. The longest of these rivers are the **Diamantina** and **Cooper's Creek.**

NO. 15. THE AUSTRALIAN ALPS.

This illustration shows part of the same district as is given in picture 25. The whole region is sometimes called the "Roof of Australia" because of its height above sea-level. The distant peak at the left of the picture is Mt. Koskiusco (see p. 18).

NO. 16. AUSTRALIAN IRRIGATION WORKS.

For the importance of irrigation in Australia see p. 21 and the top of p. 32. This picture shows the construction of some irrigation works at Burrinjuck, near Canberra (see p. 42). It is estimated that the construction of a dam across the Murrumbidgee here will render fertile over 2000 square miles of land hitherto barren.

No. 17.   AN ARTESIAN WELL.

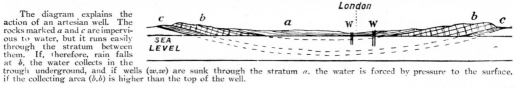

The diagram explains the action of an artesian well. The rocks marked *a* and *c* are impervious to water, but it runs easily through the stratum between them. If, therefore, rain falls at *b*, the water collects in the trough underground, and if wells (*w,w*) are sunk through the stratum *a*, the water is forced by pressure to the surface, if the collecting area (*b,b*) is higher than the top of the well.

No. 18.   FIRST TRAIN OF THE INTERCOLONIAL RAILWAY LEAVING KALGOORLIE.
(Reproduced by permission from the Railway Magazine.)

Refer to the top of p. 22. This first train to cross the continent left Kalgoorlie on 25th Oct. 1917. The Intercolonial Railway is on the 4 ft. 8½ in. guage; but the line on the left of the picture, which is on a guage of 3 ft. 6 in., belongs to the railway which links Kalgoorlie with Perth and Fremantle (refer to p. 49).

Often these streams, through lack of rain, dry up or become merely a string of brackish pools. Lake Eyre itself is not always a great expanse of water, as you might imagine from what you see marked on the map. In dry seasons it becomes a mere marsh or a waste of saltish mud, dotted here and there with shallow pools; and it is only at intervals that enough moisture is received to convert these into a single sheet of water. The whole district, therefore, is largely a barren waste, and fresh water can often be obtained only by boring wells (refer to picture 17). But to the south-east of this inland-drainage region lie the plains through which flow the Murray and Darling and their tributaries. The plain between the upper Murray and the Murrumbidgee is called the **Riverina,** and in it thousands of sheep find pasture. Even the streams of the Murray-Darling system sometimes suffer from lack of water, although they are fed by the rain and melting snows of the Dividing Range. However, water can be obtained from wells in many parts of this district, and it has become an important part of Australia not only for sheep-rearing, but also for agriculture. At the same time the variation in the volume of these rivers, and the fact that much of their water is needed for irrigation, greatly lessen their value for navigation. Sometimes they are too shallow for any but small boats. It is also impossible for cargo-carrying vessels to enter the mouth of the Murray from the sea. Just before the river reaches Encounter Bay it flows into the shallow Lake Alexandrina which Sturt discovered. This lake is separated from the sea by a sand-bar. Even Sturt's boat, which was only twenty-five feet long and of very shallow draught, could not cross this bar; so you can realise that no ocean-going vessel can sail up the mouth of the Murray. In short, it is easy to see that Australia is not well provided with inland water-ways. In this respect the continent affords a great contrast with North America, which has a splendid system of navigable rivers and lakes. By the help of them it was possible to explore and colonise this continent. But the Australian rivers, for the most part, are of no great use as waterways, and some are hardly sufficient to maintain adequate supplies of fresh water.

(iii.) West of the central lowland region which has just been described there is a huge table-land which occupies about half of the entire continent. Much of it consists of desert, covered with sand or stones and almost devoid of vegetation. Here and there are mountain ranges or inland lakes the size of which varies considerably from time to time. In the south, along the northern shores of the Great Australian Bight, are the **Nullarbor** or treeless **Plains.** This is a terribly barren region. An explorer named Eyre (after whom the lake was named) managed to cross it in 1840 from Adelaide to Albany in south-eastern Australia; but in doing so he nearly died of thirst and weariness. Quite recently, however, a railway has been built across these Nullarbor Plains so as to link up the eastern and western sides of Australia.

V.—THE CLIMATE OF AUSTRALIA.

WE can gather from what has been said about the river-systems of Australia that many parts of the continent suffer from lack of rainfall. We must now go on to consider why this is and to discuss the question of the Australian climate generally.

(i.) During the months when the Northern Hemisphere has its winter the parts of the earth's surface which receive the sun's rays at right angles at noon always lie somewhere south of the Equator. This condition is on the Equator itself at our Autumn Equinox (22nd September), and then moves southward until it reaches the Tropic of Capricorn on 21st December —the southern solstice—which is midsummer day in the Southern Hemi-sphere. After this it moves back again towards the Equator and crosses it once more on 21st March, our Spring Equinox. The northernmost point of Australia (Cape York) reaches almost to within ten degrees—say 700 miles—of the Equator, and the Tropic of Capricorn cuts across the continent very nearly in its centre. This means that the northern half of Australia will receive the greatest amount of heat from the sun between the end of September and the end of March. It takes a little while for the land-mass to get heated up as the sun's overhead position at noon moves southwards, and therefore the hottest months in Australia will tend to be January and February. For a similar reason July and August are usually the hottest months with us. But the heating of the northern part of Australia during the early part of the year causes an area of low pressure, and the winds are drawn in towards the interior. Many of these winds have crossed the warm equatorial seas and have picked up moisture on their way. When they meet the northern edge of the continent or rise over the heated low-pressure region their temperature falls, and they give up moisture in the form of rain. Thus northern Australia receives a heavy summer rainfall. Its causes are similar to those of the monsoon rainfall which deluges south-eastern Asia during the northern summer.* During the three months of December, January, and February, Darwin, on the north coast of Australia, receives 40 inches of rainfall; and that is more than Manchester, in one of the wettest parts of England, receives during the whole year.

But during the time that the sun is overhead at noon somewhere north of the Equator, Australia has its cool season. The tendency now is for the winds to move out from the continent towards the hotter regions farther north. As these winds blow from the land they are dry, and therefore there

* See *Asia in Pictures*, pp. 14 and 71.

No. 19.   LAKE HART.

This is one of the salt lakes, with no outlet to the sea, which are characteristic of the desert region of Australia. Lake Hart lies to the south of Lake Eyre (pp. 17 and 21). Notice the salt-bush in the foreground, the camels (see top of p. 18), and the hard sandstone head-land projecting into the lake.

No. 20.   A SCENE IN CENTRAL AUSTRALIA.

The man shown here is a surveyor employed in prospecting the route for the transcontinental railway (see pp. 21 and 22, and picture 18). Notice the characteristic red soil (compare picture 26), and the scanty vegetation.

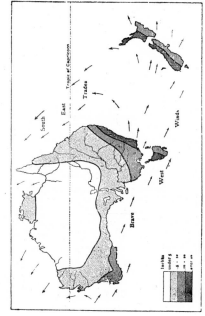

No. 21.   Average July Temperature.

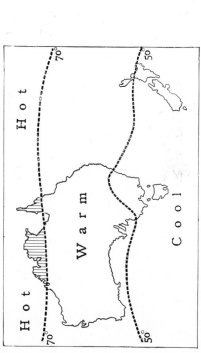

No. 22   Winds and Rainfall—May to October.

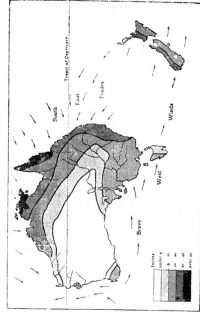

No. 23.   Average January Temperature.

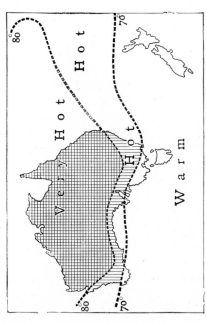

No. 24.   Winds and Rainfall—November to April.

These maps are explained in Chapter V.   The lines which join places with the same average temperature are called *isotherms*.   Notice how in summer (January) they show that land is hotter than sea in the same latitudes, while in winter (July) the reverse tends to be the case.   Notice also how the rainfall decreases from the coasts towards the interior of Australia, and how both Tasmania and New Zealand have their heaviest rainfall on the west side.

is little rain over northern Australia at this time of year. At Darwin, for example, there is, as a rule, hardly any rainfall at all during the months of June, July, and August.

We can thus distinguish as our first climatic division of Australia the **northern monsoon region** which has heavy rains during the southern summer but very little rain during the rest of the year.

(ii.) On the east coast of Australia there blows a south-east trade wind. It tends to be strengthened in summer (*i.e.* November to February), when the interior of the continent is heated up and the air is drawn in. Along this coast also a warm current in the sea flows towards the south. When the south-east winds blow towards the shore they have to cross this current; as they do so, their temperature rises and they pick up more moisture. But when they reach the barrier of the Dividing Range they are forced to rise, and a heavy rainfall is the result. At Brisbane, for example, thirty-six inches of rain fall during the six months from December to May; and that is twice as much as is received at this place during the other half of the year. It should be noticed that when the south-east trades have deposited their rain on the east side of the Dividing Range, they will pass on farther west as dry winds.

The second climatic division of Australia, therefore, is the region along the **east coast** where the **south-east trade winds** blow on shore. Here there is some rainfall all the year round, but it occurs chiefly during the southern summer.

(iii.) To the south of the belt of south-east trades there is a region of westerly winds. They correspond in the southern hemisphere to the prevailing westerlies of the northern hemisphere which bring rain to the British Isles. But the southern part of Australia comes under the influence of these west winds only when they swing northwards during the southern winter. Hence it is at this time of the year that this part of the continent receives the greater part of its rainfall. Albany, for example, in the extreme south-west of Australia, has five times as much rain during the months of June, July, and August, as it receives from December to February. A climate of this kind is called "Mediterranean," because the southern part of Europe also, for similar reasons, has the bulk of its rain in winter. It should, of course, be always remembered that the winter months of the northern hemisphere are the summer months of the other half of the world.

The third climatic division, therefore, is the region of **Mediterranean climate**. This includes the **extreme south-west** corner of Australia and the **south-eastern** parts occupied by Victoria and southern New South Wales.

26

No. 25.   THE MONARO PLAINS.

    These pasture-lands lie among the ridges of the Dividing Range, near the source of the river Murrumbidgee. The view looks
westwards and in the distance the Australian Alps can be seen. Notice the red soil, the fences to prevent the sheep from straying,
and the scanty vegetation on the hill-slopes.

Percy F. S. Spence

No. 26.   A FERTILE SPOT IN CENTRAL AUSTRALIA.

    Refer to the bottom of p. 31 and to p. 32. The picture shows that even in the dry interior of Australia there are places where vegetation
is not altogether lacking. Here and there are clumps of eucalyptus interspersed with an undergrowth of scrub. The scene illustrated is
near Alice Springs, on the Overland Telegraph route. Notice the camel caravan.

(iv.) The island of Tasmania lies so far south that it receives the south-westerly winds throughout the year. The rainfall of Tasmania, therefore, is similar to that of the British Isles. The bulk of it falls on the western side, but no part of the island lacks moisture. The following table will help to illustrate this fact:—

	WEST SIDE OF TASMANIA. MONTGOMERY. (Rainfall in inches)	EAST SIDE OF TASMANIA. HOBART. (Rainfall in inches)
December—February	9	5
March—May	8	5
June—August	12	6
September—November	15	7
Annual	44	23

Compare this with the rainfall of two towns in the British Isles which are similarly placed:—

	WEST SIDE OF BRITISH ISLES. FALMOUTH. (Rainfall in inches)	EAST SIDE OF BRITISH ISLES. LONDON. (Rainfall in inches)
December—February	12	5
March—May	9	5
June—August	9	7
September—November	14	6
Annual	44	23

Tasmania, therefore, forms by itself a fourth climatic division of Australia. It is a region of **prevailing westerly winds** which bring a fairly heavy rainfall all the year round to the western side of the island.

(v.) A cold current flows northwards along the west coast of Australia. If, therefore, winds blow from the sea here they will be cool, and will tend to increase their temperature as they pass over the land. Instead of giving up moisture they will pick it up; instead of bringing rain they will be dry winds. This is one reason why the westerly parts of Australia have a scanty rainfall. But it is not only these west winds which bring little rain. As we have already seen, those which blow from the north during the summer months give up their moisture along the northern shores of the continent; while those which come from the east have shed much of their moisture on the Pacific side of the Dividing Range. Thus the rainfall of central and western Australia is slight, and it tends to decrease as you go inland. The amount of rain actually received varies very much from time to time, but it is never large or lasting. Some parts of central Australia are practically rainless, and the heat there in the summer months is often terrific. When Captain Sturt made his journey across central

Australia the heat so much expanded the screws in his boxes and the leads in his pencils that they cracked the wood and dropped out; and he found it practically impossible to write with a pen because the ink dried up almost immediately on the nib.

The fifth and last climatic division of Australia, therefore, comprises the **interior** and **western** parts of the continent. No part of it has a good rainfall, and many parts are **practically rainless** and subject to very **high temperatures**. It contains large tracts of desert, and, as we have seen, much of it even to this day remains unexplored.

VI.—THE VEGETATION OF AUSTRALIA.

As we might have expected, the vegetation of the different parts of Australia is determined largely by the climate. We can, therefore, divide the continent up into vegetation regions which correspond roughly to the climatic divisions described in the last chapter.

(i.) In the region of great heat and heavy summer rainfall in the north there are **tropical forests** near the coasts. Palms and bamboos flourish, and there are some valuable trees such as the sandalwood, the timber of which has a pleasant perfume. The forests are often overgrown with a tangle of vines and creepers, and so form a dense mass which is difficult to penetrate. But on the landward side of this forest region the rainfall is less heavy. Here, therefore, the vegetation changes somewhat. The trees grow singly or in clumps, or along the courses of rivers. Many of them belong to the species called eucalyptus or "gum-trees." They are very common all over Australia, and it is from one variety of them that the medicinal oil, used for curing colds, is extracted. As a protection against the heat, these trees spread their leaves edgeways to the sun so as to reduce evaporation. They also shed their bark instead of their leaves. Open country, dotted with trees, is found not only on the south side of the forest region of northern Australia, but also in many other parts of the world where the rainfall is chiefly in summer and there is also a period of drought which lasts several months. It is known as **savana**, and it occurs in South America, in the Sudan, and also on the fringes of the Kalahari Desert in Africa. In many of these places the savana has proved suitable for pasturing flocks and for agriculture; but in the case of Australia this region up to the present has been very little occupied and developed. All the same it has great possibilities, and may one day become a prosperous and important part of the continent.

(ii.) On the seaward side of the Dividing Range there are also **forests** due to the rain which is received during the greater part of the year. Here

NO. 27.   PINE-APPLE FIELD, QUEENSLAND.

Pine-apples grow very well in northern Queensland, and sometimes attain a weight of as much as 20 or 30 lbs. Notice that these fruits, together with bananas, sugar, maize, and almost every plant which is of greatest use to mankind, are not native to Australia but have been introduced by colonists.

NO. 28.   AN AUSTRALIAN VINEYARD.

Refer to pp. 31 and 41. This shows a view in the Mildura district of Victoria where the vines are cultivated with the help of irrigation. Wines of the Burgundy type, such as the "Emu" brand, are imported from Australia into this country.

NO. 30.   A BUSH VALLEY IN NEW SOUTH WALES.

This is a scene in the temperate forest region of eastern Australia (see bottom of p. 28). The trees are one of the numerous varieties of eucalyptus; their height can be judged by comparison with the human figures in the foreground. On either side of the valley rise sheer limestone crags.

NO. 29.   COCO-NUT PALMS IN NORTHERN QUEENSLAND.

These trees are found on the coast-lands in all the tropical parts of Australia, and the preparation of copra (see p. 59) is an important industry. The men in the picture are Kanakas (p. 41). Notice the clusters of coco-nuts among the feathery branches at the top of the palms, and the clump of pine-apple plants at the left-hand side of the picture.

again many varieties of the eucalyptus tree are found, as well as the acacia—usually known in Australia as "wattle"—one kind of which has a beautiful yellow flower. The rainfall makes it possible to grow cultivated plants of many kinds along the coastal plain. But since this plain stretches from north to south for some hundreds of miles, the vegetation varies greatly according to latitude. In the north sugar-cane grows, as well as rubber, coffee, tea, cocoa, rice, and other tropical plants. The coconut tree (picture 29), and fruits such as the banana and pine-apple (picture 27) also flourish in this region. Farther south, along the coasts of New South Wales, maize and wheat are found, and oranges are grown—especially in the Paramatta district near Sydney.

(iii.) The **Mediterranean** regions in the south-east of Australia, and at the extreme south-west corner, can grow plants similar to those which are found in the Mediterranean countries of Europe. The vine and the olive are both cultivated in Victoria; while the district round Mildura, on the Murray, is noted for peaches and apricots which are grown with the help of irrigation from the river. In this region sheep also are reared. In the extreme south-west of Australia wheat is cultivated, as well as the vine and other Mediterranean fruits. Here also there are forests of karri and jarrah. These are two more varieties of the eucalyptus tree; they each grow to a great height and yield a hard red wood which is much used for building purposes and for paving roads in busy cities. Jarrah wood is also employed in making piles, because it does not easily rot in water, whether fresh or salt.

(iv.) The vegetation of Tasmania, as we might have expected, is not altogether unlike that of the British Isles. On the wetter west side there are dense **forests**. In the old days there was a convict station at Port Macquarie on this side of the island, and occasionally prisoners escaped from it, and tried to find their way back to Hobart. But although the distance is only about a hundred miles, very few succeeded in their attempt; the majority perished miserably among the mountains and forests. On the eastern side of Tasmania there are good pasture-lands and many orchards of apples, pears, and other fruit.

(v.) The vegetation of the different parts of the interior of Australia varies very much according to the amount of rainfall which is received. The country on the west side of the Dividing Range is in a "rain-shadow" —i.e. it is on the opposite side of a mountain-mass to that which receives most of the rain. In this part of Australia, therefore, the rainfall is less than along the Pacific coast, and it also tends to be somewhat uncertain. None the less, there are large tracts of **grassland** here and they are suitable for rearing sheep. In times of drought the flocks may suffer terribly from thirst, and thousands of animals may perish. Fortunately, in many parts of this lowland region, north of about 30° S. latitude, it is possible to tap underground water by sinking wells and so to supply drinking-water for the sheep even in dry seasons. By means of these wells, also, it is possible to carry on agriculture, and the Murray and its tributaries are also used for irrigation. In this way wheat can be grown in some places; but in other parts of this region, where the rainfall is scanty and there is no other supply of water, the country is little better than a desert or is covered with mallee scrub. This consists of a tangle of dwarf eucalyptus bushes through which it is difficult to penetrate. Farther towards the west or centre of Australia the rainfall is even scantier and more uncertain. In some parts nothing at all will grow, but elsewhere there are prickly evergreen bushes, such as the mulga scrub which is composed of thorny acacias. Another plant typical of this region is the spinifex, which is a kind of grass with hard, stiff, sharp-edged leaves. Plants like these cause painful wounds to explorers and their beasts of burden, and they afford an additional reason why travelling is difficult in the interior of Australia. Occasionally there are patches of thin, coarse grass or of salt-bush upon which sheep can feed; but for the most part there is little to support life in this hot and dry region of Australia. If, however—as occasionally happens—some rain falls, the ground which has hitherto been brown and parched may become carpeted with grasses and flowers; but they spring to life only to wither again in a very short time.

VII.—THE ANIMALS OF AUSTRALIA.

AUSTRALIA has remained cut off from the rest of the world for so long that it has kept a number of native animals which are no longer found elsewhere. For example, the platypus or duck-bill, which is found nowhere outside Australia, has proved rather a puzzle to naturalists. It is a small, furry creature, about 20 inches long, and lives in burrows along the banks of rivers. Like a duck, it has a flat beak and webbed feet and it also lays eggs; but when the young are hatched they live on their mother's milk, like new-born animals. Another class of Australian animals are the marsupials, who carry their young ones in a pouch. There are a few species of these found in America, but the great majority are peculiar to Australia. They vary in size from the red kangaroo, which is over 6 feet high, to the kangaroo rat which is only a few inches long. Other marsupials are the wallaby and the wombat, which is something like a pig and lives underground. There is also the koala or "native bear," which is hunted for its fur, and the opossum which climbs trees carrying its young ones on its back.

(*a*) Emu.
(See p. 35.)

(*b*) Lyre-Bird.
(See p. 35.)

(*c*) Kangaroo. (See p. 32.)

(*d*) Platypus, or Duck-Bill. (See p. 32.)

(*e*) Opossum. (See p. 32.)

No. 31. Some Typical Birds and Animals of Australia.

34

No. 32.   MINING PROSPECTORS.

The prospectors (see pp. 36 and 39) are ranging the open country looking for signs of gold, and are now resting in the shade of a eucalyptus tree.   They are heating water for tea in a "billy," such as is carried by the "sundowner" shown in picture 1.

No. 33.   MOUNT MORGAN MINES, QUEENSLAND.

Refer to p. 39.   The original Mount Morgan from which the mines take their name is seen in the background, behind the chimney stacks, but part of it has been quarried away.   The gold-bearing ore is crushed by machinery, and the metal extracted by a chemical process. More than a thousand men are employed at these mines.

Many of the Australian birds, like the animals, are peculiar to the continent. Some of them have wings but cannot fly; examples are the emu, found in the central plains, and the cassowary of Queensland and New Guinea. However, they can run very swiftly and soon outdistance a pursuer. The emu is often hunted because of its habit of breaking down the wire fences which surround the sheep-runs. As a result it is fast dwindling in numbers. In Tasmania it is already extinct. Other native Australian birds are the black swan, which gave its name to the Swan River in Western Australia, and the bower-bird, which, at the mating season, builds for itself a little arbour and adorns it with feathers, pieces of coloured rag or bright metal, flowers, or any other attractive object that he can find. Some Australian birds, such as the lyre-birds, parrots, and parrakeets have very beautiful plumage, but few of them can sing. It is the absence of singing-birds that strikes an Englishman most when he first enters an Australian forest. At the same time, Australian birds often have very curious cries; there is a kind of kingfisher, the kookaburra (see title page), which is some-times called the "laughing jackass" because of the noise which he makes.

Australia possesses many varieties of snake, although none of them are as dangerous as those of the Indian jungle, and many are not poisonous at all. Insects—and particularly ants—are a plague in most parts of the continent. The bull-dog ant is noted for the bites which he can give; while the termite, or white ant, is responsible for an immense amount of destruction owing to his fondness for eating wood (refer to page 18). Houses in some parts of Australia have to be built carefully on a brick or cement foundation for fear lest the termites should eat their way into the joists and floor-boards and furniture.

The fact that Australia has many animals and birds which are found hardly anywhere else, has led naturalists to enquire where exactly the line should be drawn to separate them from those of the rest of the world. A scientist named Wallace spent eight years (1854-1862) in the Malay Archipelago, just north of Australia, and as the result of his observations he decided that if a line were drawn between the islands of Bali and Borneo on the one hand, and Lombok and Celebes on the other, then the typical Australian animals and plants would all be found on the south and east side of it. This boundary, which separates the realm of Australian animals from all others, is called **Wallace's Line**. Other naturalists have since come to the con-clusion that a fixed and definite line can hardly be drawn with perfect certainty; but the fact remains that many of the animals—and plants, too—of Australia and the islands just north of it, form a class by themselves. The phrase "a 'possum up a gum tree" sums up this peculiarity.

The native Australian animals are on the whole of little value to man.

Of few of them is the skin or flesh of much use, although some kinds of opossum are hunted for their fur and the kangaroo's tail can be made into soup. When, therefore, the Europeans first settled in Australia they soon began to introduce useful animals from other lands, and most of these throve in their new home. There are now many thousands of sheep and cattle and horses in Australia, and we have already seen how useful the camel can be in the dry regions of the interior. Other European animals have not proved so valuable. The rabbit, being free in Australia from its natural enemies, such as the weasel and stoat, multiplied so quickly that it soon began to make great depredations upon the vegetation, and to deprive the sheep of their pasture. The Australians were at their wit's end to know how to put a stop to this plague, which threatened their most important industry. At first, attempts were made to poison the rabbits; but the chief result was to kill off many of the native birds and animals, while the intruders remained as lively as ever. Then scientists tried to spread a disease among the rabbits, but this also was not successful. At last a better method was adopted. The pasture-lands were enclosed with rabbit-proof wire-netting, and this area was gradually extended. Meanwhile the rabbits were hunted down and killed, and at present they are confined, more or less, to the districts which are less suitable for pasture. There they are trapped in large numbers and their carcases are exported in a frozen state. Their fur is also made into felt; so that, although rabbits are still often a nuisance in Australia, they no longer seriously threaten the prosperity of the wool-producers, and they can even be made to yield some profit.

VIII.—THE MINERALS OF AUSTRALIA.

AUSTRALIA is rich in minerals of many kinds. Chief of them is gold which is found in many parts of the continent, and is now one of its chief exports. It was first discovered in Victoria in the year 1851. At that time there were comparatively few Europeans in Australia, and the only important industry was the rearing of sheep for the sake of their wool. But as soon as it became known that there was gold in Victoria, hundreds of prospectors from all parts of the world poured into the country. Some of the miners made immense fortunes in a very short space of time. But others were not so lucky, and many men who had come to seek for gold were forced eventually to settle down to other less exciting occupations. Most of the early prospectors had worked by themselves or in bands of two or three, and they were content to collect only the gold which was found in the sediment of rivers or near the surface of the ground. This was a wasteful way of getting gold, and the available supplies soon gave out. It became necessary, therefore, to sink deep mines and to extract the metal from its

GOLD WASHING.

Refer to the bottom of p. 36. The picture shows some of the methods used by the earlier miners in order to wash the gold ore out of the earth in which it was found.

No. 34.   HYDRAULIC MINING.

By this method a strong stream of water is directed against the soil which contains gold. The force of the water washes away the dross and leaves behind the heavier particles of gold. This method of mining is much less often employed in Australia nowadays than that which is illustrated below.

No. 35.   AT WORK IN A VICTORIAN GOLD-MINE.

This photograph was taken 4154 feet below the surface of the earth. Notice the powerful drill worked by compressed air. Cartridges are placed in the holes made by this drill and the rock is then loosened by blasting. The rock is afterwards crushed and the gold extracted by a chemical process (see picture 33).

No. 36. A "STATION" HOMESTEAD.

Refer to p. 40. Of course it is only the richer sheep-farmers who can maintain so magnificent a homestead as that shown in the picture. Notice the irrigated garden and the verandahs to guard against the fierce summer heat. The squatter and his family usually spend a holiday in the hills or on the sea-coast during the hottest part of the year, after the shearing is over.

No. 37. A SHEEP-RUN.

In the Northern Territory, which is at present little developed (see p. 28), it is not unknown for a single sheep-run to be as large as the whole of Wales. Even in the more settled parts of Australia there are runs which cover an area equal to that of the county of Kent.

ore by complicated processes (see picture 35).   After a few years the gold-rush to Victoria began to decline, and ever since the mines there have been worked by large companies, which use expensive machinery for crushing the hard quartz rock which contains the gold.   The miners now work for wages and no longer prospect on their own account.   Thus Victoria still produces large quantities of gold, and the towns of Ballarat and Sandhurst (or Bendigo) are the centres of this mining industry.

In Queensland gold is found in many places.   At Mount Morgan, in particular, there are enormous deposits of this metal.   The place was originally owned by a shepherd; but two prospectors—brothers named Morgan—who happened to be visiting him noticed signs of gold, and they bought his sheep-run for a very low price.   Within a few years the district was one of the richest gold-fields in the world; and where formerly there was a strip of bare pasture-land, there is to-day a flourishing mining community (see picture 33).

Even the desert region of Western Australia has attracted settlers because of the gold which is found in some parts of it.   In the early "nineties" of last century this metal was discovered in the district where the towns of Kalgoorlie and Coolgardie now stand.   There was another "rush" to the diggings, and some of the miners walked there all the way from the coast, through the trackless desert.   But much money had to be invested before gold-mining could be successfully carried out in such a waterless waste.   Soon, in spite of the lack of water and timber, settlements were made and large towns sprang up.   Most of the necessities of life are now sent by the railway which connects this mining region with the towns on the west coast; and the water-supply is pumped for over 300 miles through a pipe line from a reservoir near Perth.

Of the other minerals in Australia coal is important.   It is found—as the name leads us to expect—near Newcastle, to the north of Sydney.   As this town lies on the coast it has become important as a coaling-station for steamers, and as a place for exporting coal.   In some parts of this district the coal crops out on the hillsides, and thus can be worked without the necessity for sinking deep shafts.   Copper, again, is mined in South Australia, near Spencer Gulf, as well as in the western part of Tasmania.   At Cobar, in New South Wales, also, there is a great copper mine; and at Mount Morgan, in Queensland, copper is now obtained in addition to gold.   At Broken Hill, in the west of New South Wales, there are rich supplies of silver and lead; and these metals, as well as tin, are mined also in Queensland and Tasmania.   Iron is found in several parts of the continent, but until recently it was not worked to any great extent.   Just before the war some large steel works were set up on the coal-fields at Newcastle; but much of the iron-ore is brought by sea all the way from South Australia—

a distance of some 1500 miles.   Iron-ore, however, has also been found near Lithgow, in the Blue Mountains behind Sydney.   This place is within reach of both coal and limestone, which is used in smelting the ore.   It seems probable, therefore, that this town will become an important centre of the Australian iron industry.   At present most of the iron-goods and machinery which Australia needs have to be imported ; but farming and mining machines are made there, and it is quite possible that local industries of this kind will develop in the near future.

IX.—THE PEOPLE OF AUSTRALIA.

THE first settlements in Australia, after the visit of Captain Cook, were made on the east side of the continent.   This is one of the few parts of Australia which have a climate suitable for the growing of European plants such as were familiar to the early colonists.   When the settlers spread over into the central lowland they found huge areas suitable for pasturing sheep —another occupation to which many of the immigrants were accustomed. Thus **wool** soon became one of Australia's chief products.   In the early days the sheep-farmer, or " squatter," as he was called, pushed out with his flocks into the open plains and settled down or " squatted " wherever he found suitable pasture.   The modern sheep-farmers are still called squatters, but many of them possess thousands of sheep, and it is not unknown for one man to hold a " station," the area of which is a million acres.   Such a sheep-owner, even if he has to live at some distance from the centres of civilisation, generally manages to lead a much more comfortable life than that of the original squatters (refer to picture 36).   He has a roomy house with a broad verandah, and double roofs and walls to ward off the fierce summer heat.   Surrounding it is a pleasant garden, often irrigated from a neighbour- ing stream and well stocked with fruit.   The house is linked by telephone with the nearest town, and the owner uses a motor-car when he wants to pay a visit.   The busiest season in the year is when the shearing takes place. All the flocks have to be rounded up from every part of the station, and the animals are herded in paddocks close to the farm-house.   A party of shearers, who travel from farm to farm like threshers in this country, arrive in order to carry out the work.   On a large station where some thousands of sheep have to be clipped, the shearers and their assistants may number seventy or eighty.   The sheep are driven into an airy shed and are dealt with one by one by the shearers.   As a rule, a clipping-machine driven by electricity is used, and an expert man can shear as many as ninety or a hundred sheep in a day.   By each shearer stands a boy with a pot of tar, from which he anoints any cuts which the sheep may receive in the hurry of the operation ; but on the whole such accidents are rare, for a shearer who injured his sheep would soon cease to be employed.   Other men, called "rouseabouts," are busy driving the sheep into or out of the shed, picking up the fleeces, and packing them into bales. The wool is pressed, sometimes by a hydraulic machine, and then taken off by horse or bullock waggons to the nearest station. Thence it travels to Sydney, Melbourne, Adelaide, Brisbane, or some other port, and is shipped across the sea. Much of it comes to this country, and is made into cloth in the mills of Yorkshire. One of the finest kinds of wool is that obtained from a special breed of sheep called the merino. It lived originally in the Mediterranean region of Europe, and Spain used to be the chief country for producing merino wool. But since this type of sheep was introduced into Australia, the Spanish industry has become unimportant, and it is from the great island-continent of the Southern Hemisphere that most of the world's finest wool now comes.

In eastern and south-eastern Australia **agriculture,** as well as sheep-rearing, is important. In Victoria the vine is an important plant, and several kinds of wine are made and exported to our country (see picture 28). You have probably seen "Australian Burgundy" advertised in shops. In Tasmania there are extensive orchards, and large quantities of fruit are exported either in the raw state or in the form of jam. The island also—like Kent—has hop-gardens, and the hops are picked by the poorer townspeople who make this the occasion of their annual holiday. In South Australia, Victoria, and New South Wales there are large wheat-producing districts; grain and flour are among the most important exports of Australia. Farther north in Queensland, sugar, bananas, pineapples, and other tropical products are grown (see page 31 and picture 27), and there are also plantations of coffee and cotton; but the climate in the parts where these products are cultivated is so hot that it is not very easy for Europeans to live and work there. To meet this difficulty a certain number of Chinese and Kanakas (natives of the Pacific Islands) were introduced into these districts as labourers. But there has been a good deal of feeling in Australia against the employment of such workmen, and the importation of Kanakas, at any rate, is now forbidden. If you look at a population map of Australia, you will notice that the greater part of the inhabitants live in the east or south-east of the continent. From what has already been said, it is easy to understand the reasons for this. It is in these regions chiefly that the earliest settlements were made, and that the sheep-farming, agriculture, and mining, upon which Australia's prosperity largely depends, are still carried on. The districts where the population is densest will be found to lie round the chief ports of the southern and eastern coasts. There is a patch of comparatively dense population also in the south-west of the central desert, where the gold-mines of Kalgoorlie and Coolgardie are situated, and another along the south-west coast where the karrah and jarri grow and coal is found.   But almost all the rest of the continent is very sparsely peopled, because it consists to a large extent of unproductive desert.   Even so, there is plenty of room left in Australia for farmers and sheep-rearers.   Although the continent is nearly as large as Europe, its entire population is at present considerably less than that of London and its suburbs ; and the government of Australia is doing its best to persuade able-bodied men from this country to emigrate in order to work on its farms or sheep-runs or in its mines.

When Australia was first discovered it was inhabited by a very uncivilised race of men.   They had dark-brown skins and black hair (see picture 8), and they lived by hunting.   They were very skilful in the use of the boomerang and of a throwing-stick, something like a sling, which can send a missile for a considerable distance.   Owing to the constant fighting with European settlers and the diseases which they caught from them, the number of the Australian natives was greatly reduced ; and now the few that remain are found chiefly in the northern and central parts of the continent—*i.e.* the regions which have not yet been colonised by white men.   In Tasmania the original inhabitants were even less civilised. Their only tools were chipped pieces of stone ; and they wore no clothes and lived in thickets or hollow trees.   The early settlers in Tasmania treated them more like wild animals than fellow human beings ; and although the authorities made attempts to save them from being exterminated, these were not very successful.   By 1847 only forty-four Tasmanian natives were left, and in 1876 the last of them died.   She was an old woman, named Trucannini, and—although she did not know it—she had the honour of being, in all probability, the last living representative of the old " Stone Age " races of mankind, such as those which lived in our islands long ages ago, before the days even of the ancient Britons.

X.—POLITICAL GEOGRAPHY OF AUSTRALIA.

Australia is divided into the five states of Victoria, New South Wales, Queensland, South Australia, and Western Australia.   Each of these has its own separate parliament, but in 1901 these states, together with Tasmania, united and formed the **Commonwealth of Australia.**   Each kept its own state government to look after local business, but at the same time a Federal parliament was set up to manage affairs which concerned all the states alike—for example, taxes and customs duties, postal arrangements, and naval and military defence.   Each state sent representatives to the Federal parliament, and it was decided to build a capital for the whole Commonwealth at **Canberra,** about 150 miles south of Sydney.   Up to the present this place has not been much developed, and Melbourne is used

NO. 38. TAKING THE WOOL TO MARKET.

Refer to the top of p. 41. In the drier parts of Australia the wool is sometimes carried on camel-back to the nearest railway station. Elsewhere, if there is a river in the neighbourhood, transport by water for some distance is often possible (see picture 13).

NO. 39. PLOUGHING ON A LARGE SCALE.

This shows a scene in the wheat-growing region of South Australia. The ploughing is done during April, May, or June, and the sowing is completed by July. Harvest takes place in December. Sometimes the ears of wheat are stripped off by an ingenious machine and the straw left standing to be burnt afterwards in order to enrich the soil, or to be used as fodder.

No. 40.   WOOL FOR SALE IN A MELBOURNE SHOWROOM.

Refer to p. 41.   The bales of wool which have been brought down from the "stations" are here shown open for inspection by prospective buyers.   Wool is the most important of Australian exports.   The amount produced in 1919-20 amounted to 663,249,000 lbs. and was valued at £42,835,000.

No. 41.   BRISBANE.

Most of the houses in Brisbane are built of wood and painted white with broad verandahs to guard against the glare of the semi-tropical sun.   Many of them also, for coolness' sake, are raised above the ground on piles to secure better ventilation.   Brisbane is a low-lying city and liable to occasional floods.

as the seat of the Federal government. In 1910 the Commonwealth took over the Northern Territory, which had hitherto formed part of South Australia. It has no separate state parliament, but is controlled directly by the Federal government.

Victoria.

In area this is by far the smallest of the Australian states, but in population it is one of the greatest. The capital is **Melbourne,** which, with its ports Williamstown and Port Melbourne, stands at the head of an inlet called Port Phillip. All round the shores of this bay there are splendid beaches, where on holidays thousands of people enjoy bathing in the surf. It is quite a safe pastime unless you venture out too far. Sharks are common off the Australian coasts, but they never come into the broken water. If you want a proper swim you must confine yourself to specially enclosed bathing pools which are filled with sea-water, but into which the sharks cannot enter. Melbourne is a busy city, for it exports the gold, wool, and other products of Victoria, and it has industries such as brewing, tanning, and woollen manufactures. Not far inland from Melbourne are the gold-mining towns of **Ballarat** and **Sandhurst** (see page 39). They are also becoming important nowadays because of the agriculture which is carried on in their neighbourhood.

New South Wales.

Captain Cook gave this name to the whole eastern coast of Australia which he explored, for it reminded him of the shores of South Wales. The name is now restricted to a part of this region (see note on page 13). The capital, **Sydney,** stands on the magnificent inlet called Port Jackson, just north of Botany Bay. The entrance to the harbour is only about a mile wide, but inside the inlet spreads out like a starfish, and it is said that its coastline measures nearly 200 miles round. Sydney, therefore, has become a very famous port and the largest city in Australia; it is a naval station and is visited by trading vessels from all parts of the world. It is connected by rail with the other large towns of Australia, and it exports the products of the interior. Chief of them are wool, gold, coal, meat, and hides. In addition, Sydney has some quite prosperous manu-factures; some of the Australian wool, for example, instead of being exported, is here woven into cloth and blankets. Other important towns in New South Wales are **Newcastle,** which exports coal; **Bathurst,** the centre of a wheat-growing district; **Broken Hill,** which is near the border of South Australia and has rich silver mines; and **Albury** on the river Murray, which forms the boundary between New South Wales and Victoria. In the neighbourhood of Albury vines are grown.

Queensland.

This state occupies all the eastern side of the continent north of New South Wales. The capital, **Brisbane** (picture 41), has a fairly good harbour and exports sugar, wool, and other products of the neighbourhood. Further north is **Rockhampton,** an outlet for the districts, such as Mount Morgan (see pages 34 and 39), which produce gold or other valuable metals. Other ports are **Townsville** and **Cairns.** From them railways run up country, and thus they are able to export the copper, tin, silver, and gold which are found in northern Queensland, as well as the sugar, bananas, cotton, and similar products which can be grown in this hot climate.

South Australia.

In South Australia is included some of the desert area round Lake Eyre, and the only part of the state which has many inhabitants is in the south-east, round Spencer and St Vincent Gulfs. The chief town is **Adelaide** (picture 44), named after the wife of William IV. Its port is much used by mail steamers. There are important copper mines at **Burra Burra,** about a hundred miles north of Adelaide, and at **Moonta,** on the Yorke Peninsula between Spencer and St Vincent Gulfs.

Western Australia.

The greater part of this huge state consists of desert, and for this reason it has a smaller population than any of the other divisions which have just been described. The capital is **Perth,** on the Swan River, which has its port at Fremantle. It is connected by rail with the gold-fields of **Kalgoorlie** and **Coolgardie.** These towns are only about thirty years old, but they are already up-to-date cities, lighted by electricity and equipped with luxurious hotels. **Albany,** in the south-west on King George's Sound, has a good harbour and exports the hard woods which are grown in this neighbourhood. It is also a coaling station. Along the northern coasts of Western Australia oyster fishing is carried on. Not only are the pearls themselves collected, but the mother-of-pearl, found in the inside of the shells, is exported in large quantities.

Northern Territory.

At present this region has been very little developed, although—as was pointed out on page 28—some parts of it have great possibilities. The only town of any importance is **Darwin,** a port on the Arnheim Peninsula. It has a fine harbour and is at the northern end of the overland telegraph from Adelaide. It exports some gold and cattle; pearl-fishing and the collecting of sea-slugs (trepang) for export to China, are also carried on in the neighbourhood.

No. 42.   SURF BATHING.

The Australians as a people work hard, but their holidays are frequent, and the climate of the most populated parts of the continent makes outdoor pastimes possible almost all the year round. Besides swimming, cricket, camping, and picnicking are among the most popular holiday occupations.

No. 43.   PERTH, WESTERN AUSTRALIA.

Perth is the smallest of the five capitals (for the other four see pictures 9, 10, 41, and 44). A visitor to Perth says: "Its many fine buildings stood out in white relief against a background of foliage, whilst the beautiful river (the Swan), winding through the valley at our feet, lent an additional charm to the scene."

No. 44.   ADELAIDE.

Adelaide stands on a small river called the Torrens, at the mouth of which is Port Adelaide on the Gulf of St Vincent. It is laid out on a very regular plan and has some fine, wide streets planted with trees. Adelaide is about one-third the size of Melbourne.

No. 45.   THE PEARL FISHING INDUSTRY—PACKING SHELL.

Refer to p. 46. This shows a scene at Port Hedland on the north-west coast of Australia. Notice (i.) the shells which are being packed in boxes for export; (ii.) The pier at which coasting vessels call. The tide along these shores goes out a great distance and hence very long piers are necessary.

Tasmania.

This island is separated from the mainland of Australia by Bass Strait, which is about 200 miles wide. A large part of Tasmania consists of bleak table-lands ridged with mountains and cleft by valleys; and the western side, as we have seen, is thickly forested. But on the east there are good pasture-lands; it is here also that the apples, pears, and hops are grown. The chief town is **Hobart,** a good port in the south; while in the north is **Launceston,** on the estuary of the Tamar. The chief products of Tasmania, in addition to those already mentioned, are wool, gold, silver, tin, and timber.

XI.—COMMUNICATIONS OF AUSTRALIA.

BEFORE the states of Australia were united to form a commonwealth, duties used to be imposed on goods which passed from one state to another, and this hampered trade considerably. All these customs duties have now been abolished, although they still have to be paid on goods brought into Australia from outside. Special concessions are made in the case of British goods. But there still remains a serious hindrance to internal trade in Australia, in that the railways of Queensland, New South Wales, Victoria, and South Australia are not all of the same gauge. This means that goods sent by rail from one state to another usually have to be transhipped at the frontier, and this causes delay and extra expense. Such a handicap is particularly serious in a country which, like Australia, is not well provided with inland waterways. It is said that it would cost over a hundred million pounds to convert all the railways of Australia to one standard gauge; but it is hoped that this may gradually be effected. Apart from these difficulties of gauge, south-eastern Australia is well provided with railways, and the capitals of all the five states are now linked together by them. It has also been proposed—as we have already seen—to join Darwin to Southern Australia by a line built along the route of the overland telegraph. But since the largest and most important towns in Australia are for the most part on the coast, much of the trade between them is carried on by sea. There are many Australian steamship companies which serve these ports; and the larger ones also are visited regularly by liners belonging to some of the great British companies, such as the P. & O. and the Orient. By means of one of these steamers it is possible to travel from London to Melbourne—a distance by the Suez Canal route of 11,255 miles—in under six weeks. When the railway across the continent from Darwin has been constructed the mail communication between Britain and south-eastern Australia will be somewhat shortened.

D

XII.—NEW ZEALAND.

NEW ZEALAND comprises two large islands—**North and South Islands**—separated by Cook Strait. There is also to the south of this group **Stewart Island**, which is much smaller than either of the others and is separated from South Island by Foveaux Strait. In size New Zealand is almost as large as the British Isles, and in several other ways also we can compare this group with our own country. In fact, New Zealand has sometimes been called the " Britain of the Southern Hemisphere."

This island group, however—unlike the British Isles—lies far out in the open ocean and does not stand close to its neighbouring continent. The shortest distance between New Zealand and Australia is nearly 1000 miles, whereas the Strait of Dover in its narrowest part is only twenty-two miles across. New Zealand also lies nearer to the Equator than does the British Isles. Auckland, an important town in the North Island, is almost exactly the antipodes (see page 7) of the Strait of Gibraltar, and the southernmost part of New Zealand lies at about the same distance from the Equator as does central France.

Like the British Isles, New Zealand has its highland chiefly on the west. In the South Island, particularly, the **Southern Alps** form a backbone of mountains running right through the island and reaching their highest point in **Mount Cook** or **Aorangi**, which is not far short of twice the height of the loftiest mountain in Australia. Like the Alps in Europe, these Southern Alps have their tops covered with snow all the year round, and many glaciers start from among the peaks. Lower down there are beautiful lakes or fiords; in fact, the scenery on the west side of this island is said to be equal to that of Switzerland or Norway. The most mountainous parts of the North Island are in the south and centre. Many of the peaks (*e.g.*, Mount Egmont) are extinct volcanoes, and there are many other proofs also that forces from the interior of the earth are still very active in this region. There are large numbers of hot springs, some of which produce boiling water in which you can cook a meal. Some also have a value in curing certain diseases, and many invalids visit this " **Thermal Springs Region**," as it is called, in order to take a course of baths in the natural hot waters. Other springs, known as geysers, shoot out jets of hot water at intervals—often to a considerable height (see picture 6). In some cases you can make them active by throwing a stone or a piece of soap down the vent of the geyser. Round these hot springs are deposited the minerals which were dissolved in the heated water; they form a brilliantly shining crust, called sinter, varying in hue from the palest green to the deepest purple. There were formerly in this district two wonderful formations of sinter

No. 46.   A HOMEWARD BOUND P. & O. LINER.

    The vessel has just cleared Sydney Heads, the mile-wide entrance to Port Jackson (see p. 45), and is now turned northwards on her voyage to England. A P. & O. liner can always be distinguished by her black hull and funnels and her pea-soup coloured upper-works.

No. 47.   MOUNT COOK, NEW ZEALAND.

    Aorangi, the Maori name of this peak, means "Cloud in the Heavens." The fact that its base stands at a comparatively slight elevation above sea-level gives Mount Cook a grandeur which is unknown to many snow-capped peaks of even greater height. Notice the glaciers and snow-fields and the mountain torrent fed by melting glaciers. Refer also to picture 5.

No. 48.　　　WAIROA BEFORE THE ERUPTION OF TARAWERA.

No. 49.　　　WAIROA AFTER THE ERUPTION OF TARAWERA.

These two pictures give some idea of the changes which were wrought by the terrible eruption of Mount Tarawera in 1886. The lake is Lake Tarawera and the mountain itself can just be made out to the right of the lower picture. It is about ten miles distant on the opposite side of the lake. The township of Wairoa, shown in picture 48, was destroyed and nearly all its Maori inhabitants, who lived in thatched huts, were killed. The few Europeans in the township were more fortunate, for they all escaped with the exception of the schoolmaster, three of his children, and an English tourist. The eruption began with showers of hot stones and fireballs and was followed by a rain of mud. Then came red-hot streams of lava, which afterwards hardened and can be seen covering the ground in the lower picture. Rotorua, although quite close to the scene of the eruption, escaped with little injury.

known as the Pink and White Terraces. Each resembled a huge flight of steps or a frozen waterfall, exquisitely coloured. But in 1886 a most terrible eruption of a neighbouring mountain, Tarawera, occurred, and as a result of it both of these terraces were destroyed. Besides volcanoes of the ordinary type, New Zealand has solfataras, which are no longer active but still give out steam and gases. In other places there are eruptions of mud issuing from cones like ant-hills.

There are many beautiful lakes in this volcanic region of the North Island. The largest and one of the finest is Lake Taupo; along one side of it runs a lofty wall of cliffs from the top of which streams, in flood-time, leap head-long in an unbroken cascade into the lake below. The whole district contains so many beautiful and curious sights that it is visited by numerous tourists. Their chief centre is at Rotorua, where there are hotels and mineral baths, and motor-cars to take visitors to see the wonders of the neighbourhood.

The North Island of New Zealand, as we have seen, lies at roughly the same distance from the Equator as the Mediterranean region of Europe; and we might, therefore, have expected that it would have a Mediterranean climate, like that of south-eastern or south-western Australia (see page 25). But because New Zealand is surrounded by the open ocean its climate is more wet and temperate than would be the case if it were part of a great continent. Although the North Island receives the westerly winds and most of its rain in winter, there is no real summer drought such as occurs in Mediterranean regions. The South Island of New Zealand—like Tasmania or the British Isles—has westerly winds all the year round, and they bring heavy rainfall to the seaward side of the Southern Alps. The other side, being in a rain-shadow, is drier. The following comparison will illustrate this (refer also to page 27):—

	WEST SIDE OF NEW ZEALAND HOKITIKA. (Rainfall in inches)	EAST SIDE OF NEW ZEALAND CHRISTCHURCH. (Rainfall in inches)
December—February	30	5
March—May	29	6
June—August	31	7
September—November	21	5
Annual	119	23

The vegetation of New Zealand tends to vary, of course, according to the rainfall. The wettest parts are to a great extent forested. On the west side of the South Island there are innumerable pines and tree-ferns, such as those illustrated in picture 51. In the North Island there grows a particular kind of pine-tree called the **kauri**. It sometimes reaches a height of 150 feet and has a girth of 40 or 50 feet. The timber is extremely useful, for, if properly seasoned, it will not warp or shrink. The sap of the tree is also used for making varnishes. Much of it is obtained in a fossilised condition. When an old kauri tree has died and decayed, its gum remains behind, like a kind of amber, and can be obtained by digging. Much of this gum must have been made by trees which perished thousands of years ago. It is most valuable when obtained in this fossilised state, but some also is taken from the living trees, for it is constantly exuding in the forks of the branches. Since the trees are so tall and so thick, and since they usually have no branches springing from the lower part of the trunk, the collecting of kauri gum from the living tree is often not a very easy matter.

On the eastern side of the South Island there are plains which are sheltered from the rain brought by the westerly winds. Here, therefore, we find, not forests, but grasslands suitable for pasturage. On the **Canterbury Plains** large numbers of **sheep** are reared, and their carcases are exported to this country under the name of " Canterbury Lamb." The ships which carry the mutton are fitted with special refrigerating rooms in which the meat is frozen hard, and the men who handle it have to wear thick gloves to protect their hands from frost-bite (see picture 52). Dairying industries are also carried on in the rain-shadow region on the east side of the South Island. Agriculture, again, is becoming increasingly important, and wheat and oats are the chief crops. In the North Island Mediterranean fruits can be grown, though it is not often found possible to ripen grapes sufficiently for making wine, as is done in the Mediterranean region of south-east Australia (see page 31). Another product of the North Island is New Zealand flax, or phormium, which is really a kind of hemp. From the fibres of its long and narrow leaves very strong ropes can be manufactured ; but the process of preparing the fibre is so difficult that phormium is not of much importance outside New Zealand.

New Zealand, like Australia, has some valuable minerals. Gold is found near Auckland and also in the north-west and south of the South Island. Coal is mined on the western side of the Southern Alps. There are also less important deposits of iron, copper, silver, and tin.

In the North Island the chief town, and the capital of the whole of New Zealand, is **Wellington**. This town stands on Cook Strait, opposite to the South Island, and it has a good harbour. In size and population, however, it is surpassed by **Auckland,** which is situated on a narrow isthmus in the north. It has two harbours—one on the east and one on the west—and the two creeks reach to within a quarter of a mile of each other. The chief docks are on the east side, for the western inlet is too shallow for steamers of any size. Behind Auckland stands an extinct volcano, Mount Eden, from which a most wonderful view can be obtained (see picture 53).

TREE-FERNS.

Some of the larger black-trunked tree-ferns reach a height of 40 feet or more. Besides these giants there are many other types of ferns, some of which can be seen in the picture. Notice also that there are tree-ferns in the undergrowth in picture 50. Among the most beautiful varieties are those which are silver-fronded and which seem to have the underside of their foliage frosted.

No. 51.

F Wright

No. 50.

A KAURI FOREST.

In order to get the gum from a living tree a piece of strong line with a weight attached is first thrown over a branch and slacked out until the weight is lowered within reach. Then a rope is hauled over the branch; with its help the gum-seeker climbs up and hacks out the gum from between the forks of the branches.

56

No. 52.   FROZEN MEAT.

The men shown in the picture are wrapping the carcases of mutton in bags to keep them clean while being handled. When frozen the mutton becomes as hard as a stone and a heavy blow on it makes no impression. Besides Lyttleton, Oamaru and Timaru, ports farther south, are important places for the export of frozen meat.

Valentine & Sons, Ltd.

No. 53.   AUCKLAND.

This view was taken from the top of Mount Eden, an extinct volcano the crater of which is now used as a reservoir. We are looking northwards across the eastern or Waitemata harbour. In the background can be seen the almost circular island of Rangitoto which also contains an extinct volcanic cone.

In the South Island the principal town is **Christchurch** with its port, **Lyttleton.** They are both busy places, for they collect and export the products of the eastern plains. **Dunedin,** in the south, has goldfields in its neighbourhood and it also exports wool and meat. **Nelson,** in the north, on Tasman Bay, is another port. It is connected by rail with **Greymouth** and **Hokitika,** two towns on the western coast of the South Island. Although they are exposed to the storms which come from the west, they are useful ports because coal and gold are found in the country behind them.

New Zealand has a government of its own and is in no way connected with Australia. Just as federated Australia calls itself a Commonwealth, so New Zealand has taken the name of **Dominion.** Most of the inhabitants are white men of British descent, but nearly one-twentieth of the population belong to the native race which originally inhabited the islands. They are called **Maoris,** and unlike the "blackfellows" of Australia and Tasmania, they had attained to a high degree of civilisation long before the arrival of European settlers. They lived in strong tribes, practised agriculture, built boats, and were very skilful at carving and making weapons. They were bold and keen fighters, and many were the wars waged between them and the early settlers, before both sides settled down to live peaceably together. Originally the Maoris practised cannibalism, but they have now given this up and most of them have been converted to Christianity. They, no less than the white inhabitants of New Zealand, have a vote, and they send their own special representatives to the Dominion Parliament. Some of the Maoris have done well at the University of New Zealand, and have entered learned professions and risen to positions of importance and responsibility in their country. Of course such cases are exceptional, for most of the Maoris still live in tribes which own large areas of land out in the country and away from the towns. They are fond of sport and excel particularly at swimming. Their numbers declined steadily until about twenty years ago, when they began to increase. It seems probable, therefore, that they will not die out as the Tasmanian race did, and as it seems fated that the natives of Australia will do.

XIII.—NEW GUINEA.

THIS island lies to the north of Australia and is separated from it by Torres Strait and the Arafura Sea. If we except Australia itself, New Guinea is the largest island in the world. In the south of it is a plain drained by the navigable Fly river; but the greater part of New Guinea is taken up by a belt of mountains, running from west to east and rising in some places to considerable heights. New Guinea has a hot, wet, and unhealthy climate, for it lies close to the Equator and receives rain, especially during the

58

No. 55.　　Harvest Dance, New Guinea.

This dance takes place when the yams and bananas are ripe. The bunches of bananas can be seen displayed in front of the house in the background. The white plumes carried by some of the men denote that their wearers have slain an enemy in single combat. The women wear red plumes

No. 54.　　A Maori Chieftainess.

The chieftainess is wearing a native costume decorated with feathers, but it is usual nowadays for the Maoris to wear European clothes. Notice the beautifully carved decoration on the house in the background.

southern summer, when the winds are moving from the north towards the centre of Australia (see page 22). The greater part of the land is covered with dense forests; and this fact, together with the presence of the mountains, explains why the interior of New Guinea has hitherto been but little explored. The chief food-plants, which can be cultivated with very little trouble, are bananas, yams (a kind of sweet potato), coco-nuts, and sugar-cane. At present the island has little trade, but it would be possible to develop thriving plantations of tropical plants, and it is thought that there are important deposits of gold. The chief difficulty in the way of these industries is the lack of labourers.

New Guinea used to be divided between the Dutch, who still hold the western half, the British, who possess the south-eastern end called **Papua,** and the Germans. But upon the outbreak of war in 1914 the Australians took possession of German New Guinea; and after the war was over the Commonwealth was given a "mandate," or trust, to take charge of this territory.

There are few towns of any size or importance in the island. **Port Moresby,** on the east side of the Gulf of Papua, has a regular steamship communication with Queensland. The natives in some parts of New Guinea still practise head-hunting, and are given to cannibalism. These pursuits are being put down by the British, but it has been found more difficult to persuade the natives to work in a land where the necessaries of life can be obtained with so little trouble. The chief industries of New Guinea are gold, copper, and tin mining which are carried on by white men; and the cultivation of coco-nuts and other tropical products, for which native labourers are employed by white planters. The flesh of the coco-nut, which is found outside the kernel, is dried and exported. In this form it is called copra, and it is largely used for making soap, candles, and margarine. Copra forms one of the chief exports of New Guinea; but the fact remains that this island, although it possesses a very fertile soil and valuable minerals, has up to the present been but little developed.

XIV.—OCEANIA.

THIS name is given in a general way to all the innumerable islands of the Pacific Ocean. They have been divided into two groups according to the type of people which inhabit them; and these two divisions are known as **Melanesia** and **Polynesia.**

Melanesia.

Melanesia means "the black islands"; the name is given to those groups which lie east and south-east of New Guinea and which are inhabited by a dark-skinned and frizzly-haired race, similar to that which lives in New

Guinea itself. The original inhabitants of Australia also belong to the Melanesian race.

The greater part of the **Bismarck Archipelago** and the **Solomon Islands** used to belong to Germany, but since the war they have been entrusted to British control. The Solomon islanders are clever boat-builders, and their war canoes are wonderfully inlaid with mother-of-pearl (see picture 2). They are also skilful at catching fish by spearing them or shooting them with a bow and arrow. South of the Solomon Islands are the **New Hebrides,** which are under the joint protection, or "condominium," of Britain and France. These islands are mountainous and export copra and sugar. **New Caledonia,** together with the **Loyalty Islands** farther east, belongs to France and is used as a place of deportation for convicts. The island produces tropical fruits and sugar and also has valuable minerals. The chief port is **Noumea.**

Polynesia.

This name, which means "many islands," is given to all the small groups in the Pacific Ocean with the exception of those inhabited by the dark-skinned Melanesians. The members of the Polynesian race are of a copper-colour and have wavy hair; when they were first discovered by Europeans they were found to have reached already a considerable degree of civilisation. The Maoris of New Zealand are Polynesians.

Many of these Polynesian islands are formed of coral, and they rise from the depths of a very deep ocean. The coral is built up from the hard limy skeletons of millions of tiny creatures like sea-anemones. When they die, their soft substance decays and the hard part is left. It forms a sediment of which the coral is gradually made. The constant pounding of the waves on the edge of the coral reef piles up the rock and forms a narrow strip of beach all round, while in the centre a shallow lagoon is left. A coral island of this kind is called an **atoll.** The tree most commonly found growing on such islands is the coco-nut palm, sprung, doubtless, from coco-nuts which have floated over the sea from the coasts of some other land. Those Pacific islands which have a volcanic soil and are not built of coral are much more fertile and can be cultivated. The chief food of the inhabitants is the bread-fruit, which has to be roasted before it can be eaten.

The chief Polynesian group is the **Fiji** archipelago. Most of these islands are volcanic and therefore productive; sugar, copra, coffee, and cotton are exported. The native Fijians, like so many of the natives of tropical regions, are disinclined to work. Where nature provides food without the need of cultivation, and where the climate makes clothing unnecessary, we can hardly blame the inhabitants if they do not care to earn wages which can be

No. 56. TAI-O-HAI, MARQUESAS ISLANDS.

The Marquesas Islands lie just south of the Equator and are one of the most easterly groups of Polynesia. They belong to the French. Notice the tropical forest clothing the lower slopes of the mountains, and the traders' houses and store-rooms. The islands have a small trade in copra and cotton.

No. 57. NATIVE HOUSE, FIJI ISLANDS.

These houses are very well built. They rest upon high stone or earth foundations, and consist of a pole framework elaborately thatched with reeds, grass, and leaves. The sides are usually of reeds sewn and plaited together; the thatch is of grass and leaves fastened down by long thin rods which are secured to the rafters by split canes.

62

No. 59.   A Chief's House, New Hebrides.

You should contrast these black-skinned Melanesians with the copper-coloured Polynesian Maori shown in picture 54. The chief's hut is surrounded by a rough wall of stone and coral. The shell hanging from a pole shows that the house is "taboo" or sacred, and that no one may enter it without the chief's permission.

No. 58   A Lagoon, Solomon Islands.

This picture gives a good idea of the low and flat appearance of islands which have been built up of coral. Notice the coco-nut palms. The boat belongs to a European trader. The natives on the shore have spears with which they kill fish. Refer to p. 60.

of little benefit to them.   Most of the work on the Fijian plantations, therefore, is carried on by coolies from India who come out for a fixed period of years and then return to their native land.   The chief port in Fiji is **Suva**, which is visited regularly by steamers from New Zealand.   The group belongs to Britain.   To the north-east of Fiji lie the islands of **Samoa**, which have luxuriant forests and produce copra, cocoa, and rubber.   Part of this group formerly belonged to Germany, but since the war these islands have been entrusted to New Zealand.   Farther east are the **Society Islands**.   The chief of them is **Tahiti**, which was visited by Cook and from which the transit of Venus in 1769 was observed (see page 10). The group was named after the Royal Society of London—a scientific body which was responsible for sending out this astronomical expedition.   The Society Islands are now under French protection.

It would be a long task to mention all the Polynesian islands.   Most of them produce little besides copra or pearl-shell, or else they are important because they possess submarine cable stations.   But there remains one other group of which something must be said.   It lies away to the north, not far from the Tropic of Cancer, and is known as the **Hawaiian** archipelago.   It was formerly called the Sandwich Islands, for it was discovered by Cook on his third and last voyage in 1777, and named by him in honour of Lord Sandwich, the first Lord of the Admiralty, who had sent him upon this expedition.   But the group now belongs to the United States, and they have officially named the whole archipelago after Hawaii—the largest island which it contains.   It was here that Cook was murdered in 1779, during a dispute with the natives.   The Hawaiian Islands contain volcanoes, one of which is said to be the largest in the world, and is frequently in eruption.   The group produces sugar, rice, coffee, and tropical fruits such as pineapples ; and a considerable trade is carried on, more particularly with the United States.   The Polynesian natives of Hawaii are said to be dwindling in numbers, and, as we have seen, they do not make good workmen.   Foreign labourers, chiefly from Japan and China, are employed on the plantations. The chief town of the Hawaiian archipelago is **Honolulu**, a port of call for steamers voyaging between North America and Asia or Australia.

XV.—ANTARCTICA.

CAPTAIN COOK'S second voyage showed that if there was a great southern continent it must lie almost wholly within the Antarctic Circle.   Such a land would be an icy waste and of little value to mankind.   It was not until 1840, therefore, that any further attempt was made to explore these regions.   In that year a naval officer named Ross, who was in command of two ships, the "Erebus" and "Terror," led an expedition to the Antarctic Seas.   He sailed from Hobart and discovered a big gulf leading into the frozen continent. This was called Ross Bay, and on its shores two volcanoes—one of which was active—were discovered. To them the names of Mount Erebus and Mount Terror were given. But the land itself was rendered inaccessible by a huge ice-barrier which rose like a gigantic wall from the water's edge. Ross was unable, therefore, to explore the continent itself, and a second voyage which he made was equally unsuccessful.

Little was done after this until 1901 when Captain Scott, sailing from New Zealand, coasted along the ice-bound shores of Ross Bay. With great difficulty he managed to climb the frozen wall of the continent, and by the aid of sledges made a journey into its interior. He found everywhere a high plateau, covered with snow and ridged in some places with mountains which reached a height of 15,000 feet or more. This frozen tableland is swept continually by icy blizzards. No native inhabitants are able to support life in so inhospitable a region. There are no land animals, such as the polar bears of the Arctic regions; although the coasts are visited by many sea-birds— as, for example, penguins—and marine animals such as seals and sea-lions.

Information such as this was brought back by Scott as the result of his having made the first long land-journey on the Antarctic continent. In 1909 another expedition, under the command of Shackleton, who had been one of Scott's party, reached within ninety-seven miles of the South Pole; but blinding blizzards made farther progress impossible. Scott was again at work a few years later. On January 18th, 1912, he and four companions reached the Pole itself, but they perished amid the icy wastes on their return journey. They had been forestalled by a Norwegian explorer named Amundsen. He and his party, travelling on skis and with the aid of Eskimo dogs and sledges, had set up the Norwegian flag at the Pole only a month previously. Scott found this flag and one of Amundsen's tents still standing when he arrived.

All these explorations have shown us that the continent of Antarctica, although equal in area to Australia, is simply a lofty plateau covered with a very thick ice-sheet and often fringed by a frozen sea. It must always be difficult of access; for even in the summer, when the ice along the coasts breaks up, this floats away in the form of huge tabular bergs which make approach dangerous even for the strongest ships. Antarctica, therefore, must always remain undeveloped and even unexplored, save by such brave and hardy adventurers as those whose exploits have been described.